DEMOLITION DERBIES

The Thrill of Racing

NICKI CLAUSEN-GRACE

Rourke
Publishing LLC
Vero Beach, Florida 32964

www.rourkepublishing.com

PHOTO CREDITS: © Tootles: page 4, 9;, 20 , 22 ; © Associated Press/BARBARA J. PERENIC: page 5, 11; © Jason Merideth: page 6; 17 top; © Liz Van Steenburgh: page 8; © Associated Press/STEVE MUSCATELLO: page 10; © Associated Press/WAYNE MARIS: page 12/13;; © Associated Press/BRIAN HARKIN: page 14 top; ©Associated Press: page 16; ©Michael Stokes: page 17; ©Associated Press/DYLAN MOORE: page 18; © Benny Mazur: page 19; © Tory Schutte: page 21

Edited by Meg Greve

Cover and Interior design by Tara Raymo

Library of Congress Cataloging-in-Publication Data

Clausen-Grace, Nicki.

Demolition derbies / Nicki Clausen-Grace.

p. cm. -- (The thrill of racing)

Includes index.

ISBN 978-1-60472-368-7

1. Demolition derbies--Juvenile literature. 2. Automobile racing--Juvenile

literature. I. Title.

GV1029.9.D45C53 2009

796.7--dc22

2008011244

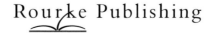

Rourke Publishing

www.rourkepublishing.com – rourke@rourkepublishing.com
Post Office Box 3328. Vero Beach. FL 32964

Table of Contents

Demolition Derbies

For most people, the screech of metal and crash of breaking glass causes fear. For **demolition** derby drivers, this is the sweet sound of success. A demolition derby, or demo, is like a gladiator fight. It is a **duel** to the death (between cars of course). Drivers line their cars up, usually in a square or rectangular arena, then try to ram into each other. The last car running is the winner.

Drivers try to wreck each other's cars in a demolition derby.

The winner is the last car that can still be driven out of the arena and has not been disqualified.

Demolition derbies are widely believed to have started at county fairs in the 1940s. People enjoyed watching drivers destroy old cars by smashing into them.

Demos drew big crowds at county fairs.

In the late 1950s, Larry Mendelsohn organized and **promoted** the first official demolition derby at Islip Speedway in New York. Since then, demolition derbies have become popular all over the world.

Auto-Bio

Larry Mendelsohn was a 28-year-old stock car driver who noticed that the fans became excited when cars crashed at races. He decided to promote the demolition derby, an event that was all about the crashes. He advertised with a newspaper ad that read, "Wanted: 100 Men Not Afraid to Die."

Driving in a Derby

Demolition drivers are masters at driving backwards! Their goal is to hit the front and sides of other cars with the backs of their cars. This way they can protect their car while damaging the important parts of other cars, such as **radiators** or wheel axles.

Thrilling Fact

Most demos have qualifying races called heats. The winners from each of the heats compete in the feature event to determine the overall winner.

Driving backwards is a good thing at a demolition derby.

Believe it or not, there are rules in demolition derbies. Drivers cannot hit other cars head-on, or on the driver's side door. The drivers' arms and legs must stay inside. They cannot work together to hit other cars. To stay in the game, drivers must hit a **live** car every 60 seconds.

A driver gets a black flag, or is disqualified, if he or she breaks certain rules or another car knocks them out of the arena.

Thrilling Fact

Drivers that only make the minimum amount of hits are sandbagging, or taking the easy way out.

Demolition derbies feature many different types of cars. Drivers buy and modify their cars, then enter them in the race that fits their style.

Full-Sized Car Derbies

Full-sized cars are the original demo vehicles. These cars are bigger and heavier with a **chassis**, or frame, and a **modifiable** body. This makes them more expensive. Some examples of full-sized cars include the Chrysler Imperial, Chevy Caprice, and Lincoln Town Car.

Full-sized cars from the 1960s and 1970s tend to be heavier and sturdier, making them demo favorites.

Compact Car Derbies

The newer compact cars feature a body with a built-in chassis. Because of this, drivers cannot modify them as much, making them cheaper to drive in a derby. The Chevy Cavalier, AMC Spirit, and Ford Pinto are all compact cars.

Special Derbies

There are many unusual types of demos. Powder Puff derbies are for women only, while other derbies feature nothing but minivans.

Thrilling Fact

Some organizers soap down the derby course so cars will go slower.

Can you picture your bus driver smashing into another bus? There are demos that pit school buses against each other. There are even demos in which a blindfolded driver receives driving instructions from a passenger who can see.

Farmers enjoy demo derbies pitting drivers in **combines**, or tractors, against each other.

It makes sense that certain cars would hold up better than other cars. Chrysler Imperials built between 1964 and 1967 are considered the best derby cars ever.

Many demos outlaw these cars because of the **advantage** they offer drivers.

Extra sturdy Chrysler Imperials built between 1964 and 1967 feature a truck chassis, an o-frame, and extremely strong steel.

The Impala is one of the best derby cars still allowed. They are full-framed and have strong steel bumpers.

Drivers say it is getting harder to find these cars for derbies.

You might imagine that it is dangerous to drive in a demolition derby. To stay safe, drivers take precautions. They wear helmets, goggles, gloves, long sleeve shirts, and pants. Some even wear neck supports.

Thrilling Fact

Some drivers put padding on the inside of their door to soften the blow of hard hits.

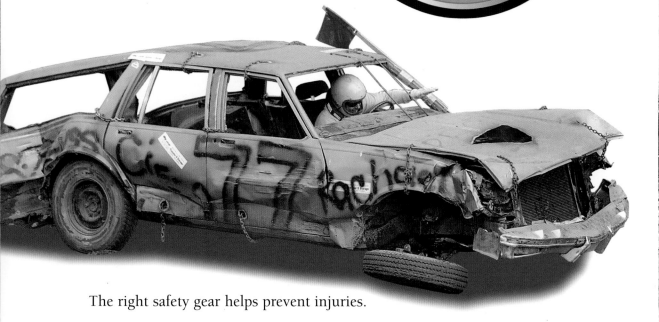

The right safety gear helps prevent injuries.

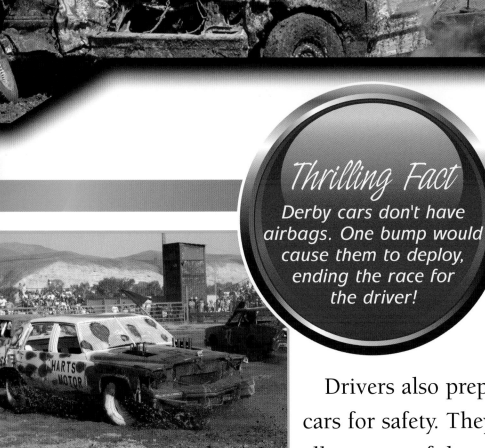

Thrilling Fact

Derby cars don't have airbags. One bump would cause them to deploy, ending the race for the driver!

Safety features of a Demolition Derby car.

Drivers also prepare their cars for safety. They remove all or most of the glass and anything **flammable**, or likely to catch fire. They replace the gas tank with a smaller fuel cell and install it inside the car for extra protection. They cut a fire hole into the middle of the hood in case they need to put out a fire. A fire extinguisher is required to be onboard.

County and state fairs all over the nation still hold many derbies. Derbies also run at circle tracks that host other types of races as well.

Demos continue to draw big crowds at county fairs.

Some derbies are much larger. For example, Demolition Events National Tour (D.E.N.T), Crash-o-Rama, and Metal Mayhem are popular demolition derbies with bigger prizes.

Many people can afford to drive in demolition derbies. A typical car might cost $200.00. The driver will spend two to three weeks and $200 to $300 getting it derby ready. The car will use less than five gallons (19 liters) of gas for a 15 to 30 minute derby.

Thrilling Fact

Some drivers get their cars free from junkyards and friends.

Most demolition derby drivers are not making a fortune with their wins. Drivers pay $20 to $200 to enter a race. Prizes range from $50 to $1,000 for many events. Some big events offer **purses** of up to $20,000 split between winners of each heat.

Auto-Bio

By day, Tory Schutte is a Navy recruiter, but on nights and weekends, you will find him grinding metal at demolition derbies. He has worked on demo cars with his brothers since he was a young child. He is in his twelfth year as a demo driver and has won 100 heats and 6 features. He is also the founder of the Demolition Derby Drivers Association (DDDA).

Putting on the Breaks

If your favorite part of stock car racing is when the drivers crash, or your favorite ride at the fair is the bumper cars, then demolition derbies are for you.

Glossary

advantage (ad-VAN-tij): something that is helpful

chassis (CHASS-ee): frame that a car is built on

combines (KOM-bines): big machines that cut grain in a field

demolition (dem-oh-LISH-uhn): to destroy by breaking apart

duel (DOO-uhl): a fight between two people using swords or guns

flammable (FLAM-uh-buhl): likely to catch fire

live (LIVE): a car that is still driving and hasn't been black flagged

modifiable (MOD-uh-fye-uh-buhl): able to be changed

promoted (pruh-MOH-ted): advertised

purses (PURSS-is): prize money

radiators (RAY-dee-ay-tur): metal devices that water flows through to cool a vehicle's engine

Index

Websites to Visit

www.cachedemoderby.com

www.en.wikipedia.org/wiki/Demolition_derby

www.auto.howstuffworks.com/

Further Reading

Marx, Mandy R. *Demolition Derby Cars (Blazers--Horsepower)*. Capstone
High Interest, 2006.

Savage, Jeff. *Demolition Derby Cars(Wild Rides)*. Capstone High
Interest, 2003.

About the Author

Nicki Clausen-Grace is an author and fourth grade teacher. She is a cautious driver who prefers watching demolition derbies from the sidelines. She lives in Oviedo, Florida with her husband Jeff, and two children, Brad and Alexandra.